ENGLAND
of One Hundred Years Ago
**PHOTOGRAPH
COLLECTION**

THE SOUTH COTSWOLDS

SELECTED BY ALAN SUTTON

ALAN SUTTON

First published in the United Kingdom in 1992
by Alan Sutton Publishing Limited
Phoenix Mill, Stroud, Gloucestershire

First published in the United States of America
by Alan Sutton Publishing Incorporated
83 Washington Avenue, Dover, New Hampshire

Copyright © Alan Sutton Publishing Limited, 1992

British Library and Library of Congress
Cataloguing in Publication Data applied for

ISBN 0-7509-0300-7

Typesetting and origination by
Alan Sutton Publishing Limited
Graphics and Design Department.
Printed in Great Britain by
Bath Colour Books.

Some blemishes have been removed by extreme enlargement of the image to individual pixel
level, with careful computer graphics surgery to mend scratches, foxing, or other damage to the
photographic image.

ENGLAND
of One Hundred Years Ago
VOLUME TWO
The South Cotswolds

The photograph collection of England of One Hundred Years Ago is an attempt to find and produce some of the best images in existence from late Victorian times up to the onset of the First World War. The country has been split into the traditional counties and this volume, numbered 2, represents the South Cotswolds in Gloucestershire.

The criteria for selection are quality and clarity in the image together with subject interest. An attempt has been made to ensure a reasonable geographical balance within the area covered, but it has to be admitted that some areas were much more photographed than others.

The printed images are intended to be used for framing, although some people may wish to buy additional separate prints for framing by using the order form at the back of the book, and to keep this book intact. If the order form becomes separated from the book please write to the Phoenix Mill address advising the volume number and plate number you require.

The reproductions in this book are obtained by digital scanning and computer enhancement. Some blemishes have been removed by extreme enlargement of the image to individual pixel level, with careful computer graphics surgery to mend scratches, foxing, or other damage to valuable photographic images. The pictures on the facing page show a scratch, enlarged and repaired. Some damage, or blemishes in an otherwise interesting photograph are beyond reasonable repair, and have been left.

The monochrome image is then further enhanced by being artificially separated and printed in a four colour process with a sepia bias. The result is a high quality image with visual depth. The finished printed image is then protected by a careful application of matt varnish to reduce fading and to add protection. The paper is a super-calendared, acid free matt art of 170 grammes weight per square metre.

The contents of the photographs remain totally genuine and the enhancement and surgery are used only to mend damage and not to create artificial images!

The pictures in this volume are the work of a number of photographers. Some are Frith photographs from the company founded by Francis Frith. Although a Surrey based company, the Friths had a connection with Gloucestershire in that Francis Frith's son, Eustace, had started a collotype printing factory at Charfield. The Frith family decided to sever their connection with this factory in 1907, and it was taken over by some of the management there, becoming the Cotswold Publishing Company. Happily, many of the original negatives survived into the 1960s, when they were saved from destruction by the farsightedness of one of the employees, Donald Emes, who has kindly lent prints taken from the original glass plates. Apart from Frith and CPC pictures, a number of other photographers were active in the area, and this collection represents a varied style of photography, although children tend to predominate, to the enhancement of the images.

In some cases, the original photographs are no longer in existence, and the only surviving images are the collotype postcard reproductions. Some of these have been used in this volume, but the result is inevitably a fall off in quality of the reproduced image. The collotype process is a continuous tone printing that produces a faithful reproduction of the original photograph, but with softened results, reducing any harshness or sharp contrast. Collotype images are reproduced in plates 11, 16 and 23; all other images are taken from photographs.

Because of the size limitation of this volume, most of the views selected are of the larger villages or market towns. Other pictures will eventually be published in future South Cotswold volumes in this series.

Contents

Acknowledgements

The photographs in this book have been lent from private and
library or museum collections. Grateful thanks go to the fol-
lowing: Donald Emes, plates 1, 18, 24, 27 and 28; David
Evans, plates 7 and 8; Stanley Gardiner, plates 3, 5, 6, 17, 21
and 22; Gloucestershire Record Office, plates 15 and 19; Wilf
Merrett, plates 2, 4, 12, 13, 14, 25 and 26; David Viner, plate
20; Matt Welsh, plates 9, 10 and 11; author collection, plates
16 and 23.

Plate 1. CARING FOR THE CLOSED MILL AND AN INDUSTRY
OF THE PAST
Monk's Mill, Alderley, *c.* 1905

Plate 2. HOPSCOTCH
Outside Avening church and school, *c.* 1908

Plate 3. THE WATER CARRIERS
Stroud Road, Bisley, *c.* 1910

Plate 4. COTSWOLD SYMMETRY
Bisley, *c.* 1915

Plate 5. THE COAL CART
A delivery of coal by donkey cart in Coppice Hill, Chalford, *c.* 1907

Plate 6. CHALFORD
Grist Mill Locks, *c.* 1918.

Plate 7. THE STUDIED POSE
The Bloodworth and Barnbrook families with baptist friends
at Coaley Quarry, *c*. 1893

Plate 8. FAMILY FRIENDS
The Bloodworth and Barnbrook families at Coaley Quarry, *c.* 1893

Plate 10. THE KING'S HEAD
Parsonage Street, Dursley, *c.* 1908

Plate 11. THE MILLS AND THE TOWN
Dursley, *c.* 1898

Plate 12. MILITANT YOUTH
The Market House, Minchinhampton, *c.* 1904

Plate 13. A REST FROM WORK
Villagers at Miserden, *c.* 1910

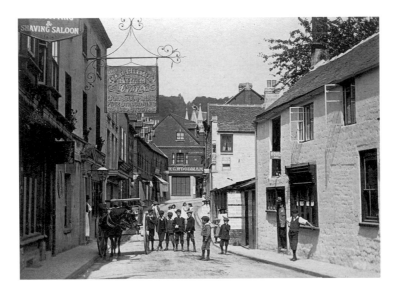

Plate 14. NAILSWORTH LADS
Children outside the Clothiers Arms, Market Street, Nailsworth, *c.* 1904

Plate 15. THE APPROACH TO THE STATION
A view looking towards Watledge, Nailsworth, *c.* 1900

Plate 16. THE ITINERANT VENDOR
The Black Horse, North Nibley, *c.* 1910

Plate 17. MARY TWISSEL
A rural view at Oakridge, *c.* 1908

Plate 18. HOOPS AND STICKS
Outside the Falcon Hotel, New Street, Painswick, *c.* 1904

Plate 19. THE STREET CLEANING PARTY
New Street, Painswick, *c*. 1900

Plate 20. THE WHARFINGER'S COTTAGE
Daneway, Sapperton, 1904

Plate 21. THE BRICKLAYERS ARMS
Daneway, Sapperton, 1917

Plate 22. SHOPPING IN STROUD
George Street, Stroud, *c.* 1900

Plate 23. A REST ON THE STEPS
Chipping Steps, Tetbury, *c.* 1885

Plate 24. UNDERNEATH THE LAMPPOST
The corner of Church, and Long Streets, Tetbury, *c.* 1900

Plate 25. THE CROSS INN
A view of South Woodchester, *c.* 1911

Plate 26. THE CARTER'S LAD
Frogmarsh, South Woodchester, *c.* 1902

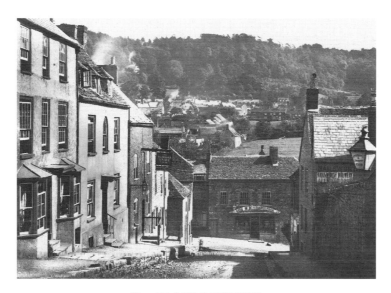

Plate 27. LUDGATE HILL
A view of Wotton-under-Edge, *c.* 1910

Plate 28. IN THE SUNSHINE FROM MARKET STREET
A view of Wotton-under-Edge looking from Long Street
into High Street, *c.* 1880